T0115526

★ ★ ★ ★ ★ The True Story Behind ★ ★ ★ ★ ★

LINCOLN'S
GETTYSBURG ADDRESS

By Jennifer Armstrong
Illustrated by Albert Lorenz

Previously published as *A Three-Minute Speech:
Lincoln's Remarks at Gettysburg*

ALADDIN
New York   London   Toronto   Sydney   New Delhi

ALADDIN

An imprint of Simon & Schuster Children's Publishing Division
1230 Avenue of the Americas, New York, NY 10020
This Aladdin hardcover edition September 2013
Text copyright © 2003 by Jennifer Armstrong
Illustrations copyright © 2003 by Albert Lorenz
Previously published as *A Three-Minute Speech:
Lincoln's Remarks at Gettysburg*

For information about special discounts for bulk purchases,
please contact Simon & Schuster Special Sales at 1-866-506-1949
or business@simonandschuster.com.
The Simon & Schuster Speakers Bureau can bring authors
to your live event. For more information or to book an event contact
the Simon & Schuster Speakers Bureau at 1-866-248-3049
or visit our website at www.simonspeakers.com.
The text of this book was set in Adobe Caslon Pro.
Manufactured in the United States of America 0813 FFG
2 4 6 8 10 9 7 5 3 1
Library of Congress Control Number 2013933919
ISBN 978-1-4424-9388-9 (hc)
ISBN 978-1-4424-9387-2 (pbk)
ISBN 978-1-4424-9389-6 (eBook)

*In grateful memory of my great-grandfather
Corporal Alfred Armstrong, New York Volunteer
Infantry 134th Regiment, who was a prisoner of
war while his comrades fought at Gettysburg and
lost two-thirds of their force—otherwise
I might not be here today.*

—J. M. A.

Four score and seven years ago,
our fathers brought forth, upon this
continent, a new nation, conceived in
liberty, and dedicated to the proposition
that all men are created equal.

CHAPTER ONE

★ ★ ★ ★ ★

IN THE BEGINNING

IN THE BEGINNING were the British colonies in North America, separated by an ocean from the land they had left behind. Over the years the colonists became less and less British and more and more something new: American. Here, a man or a woman was not judged by his family or her title. Instead they were judged by their actions. There were no lords or dukes or baronesses. Here, no family deserved more wealth or more land or more opportunity than anyone else simply because they had an aristocratic ancestor. Those ancestors were buried in the ground an ocean away. Their voices did not reach across the Atlantic to demand special treatment. Here on the American continent people earned their place.

Not only that, but the colonists felt they had earned something else: the right to decide for themselves what should happen on this side of the great ocean.

The colonists wished to create their own laws.

The king said *no*.

The colonists wished to have some say in the government that collected taxes from them.

The king said *no*.

The colonists wished to choose their own judges.

The king said *no*.

The colonists wished for this, that, and another reasonable thing. To each request the king said *no*. Picture a father snapping at his children, telling them to be quiet and go to their rooms and stop asking so many questions.

The colonists were beginning to wonder why they should continue to be ruled this way. Every child outgrows the authority of the parent. The American colonies had finally grown up. They no longer wished to be ruled by a king who was so far away he might as well live in a fairy story. It was time to make a new nation, a nation whose only parent would be freedom. This nation would steer its course by a revolutionary idea: All people were created equal. It would be a democracy, a government of the people, not an aristocracy, a government

of kings and princely lords. That was the idea the country would dedicate itself to.

This was not the sort of idea that Britain was going to sit still for. King George sent troops to knock heads together in the rebellious and troublesome colonies. America knocked back.

On July 4, 1776, America officially declared itself to be independent of Britain, but it took years of deadly war to make that independence a reality. At last, in 1783, the British sailed away from the new United States of America, and the war was over.

This new nation had been born in a storm of bullets and cannon fire, and Americans had pulled together with united hearts in the wartime emergency. But now it was time to see what kind of nation it was when the emergency was over. A Union of free states. What a grand idea! What kind of place was it going to be, where all men were created equal?

What kind of—but wait. Back up a moment. All men were created equal?

What about the slaves?

★ ★ ★ ★ ★

A PECULIAR INSTITUTION

THE AMERICAN CONTINENT was a horn of plenty. Great herds of animals roamed its plains and threaded through the forests. In the rivers and ocean bays, sunlight gleamed silver off the scaly fins of countless fish. The earth was rich. Plant a seed, and behind your back a tree would grow as you walked away. In the Northern states vast forests supplied the trees and timber for ships, and the fuel for factories

and towns. Settlements were close together. Farms were small. Merchants traded for thick furs from the cold woods. In the busy ports the wharves were clogged with imported furniture and pottery and fine cloth from Europe and the lands of distant Asia.

In the Southern states farmers spread out thinly across the broad land. Tobacco, cotton, and rice grew green and rustling in the warm air. Immense plantations of crops required immense numbers of cheap farmhands to do the sowing, weeding, and harvesting. By the time of the American Revolution, the Southern states relied heavily on slave labor.

At the time that the colonies were preparing to declare independence and form a new government, the question of slavery arose. Perhaps slavery could be eliminated over time, suggested some of the founding fathers from the North.

After all, what good is all this talk of equality if half our colonies rely on slave labor? But some of the founders from the South threatened that any discussion about discouraging the slave trade would drive them out of the room. End of discussion. You can declare independence on your own, but leave us out of it. Phasing out slavery would mean ending a whole way of life: The Southern states had *no* interest in doing *that*.

The most they could all agree upon in those revolutionary days was that they wouldn't allow slavery in any of the new territories beyond the frontier. As long as slavery was permitted to stay where it already existed, the Southern states would go along with the plan. So in order to speak out against Britain with a unified voice, the founders decided to leave the question of slavery alone.

The first paragraph of the new country's statement of goals, the Constitution, read, "We the People of the United States, in Order to form a more perfect Union . . . and secure the Blessings of Liberty to ourselves and our Posterity do ordain and establish this Constitution for the United States of America."

"Blessings of Liberty" sounded pretty impressive and noble. The authors of the Constitution made no mention of slavery. Neither did the authors of the Declaration of Independence.

For eighty-seven years—four score and seven years—the United States of America tried to make believe that it really and truly was a nation where all men were created equal and enjoyed the blessings of liberty.

But eventually, the make-believe had to end.

★ ★ ★ ★ ★

CHAPTER THREE

THE PRESSURE

NOT EVERYONE WAS in on the make-believe, of course: Women weren't allowed to vote. They knew *they* weren't included in "all *men* are created equal." That wouldn't be fixed until 1920. And the native people of America who were being pushed farther and farther west weren't included either. That injustice would take many years to repair too.

But to return to the problem of slavery: Many

people, mostly in the Northern states, argued for the abolition of slavery. Abolish it! Put an end to this "let's pretend" equality and stand true equality in its place. The abolitionists put constant pressure on the government of the United States to outlaw slavery. It was cruel. It was barbaric. It was not worthy of a civilized nation. And it mocked our Constitution and its blessings of liberty.

The abolitionists weren't the only ones who wanted to do away with slavery. The slaves themselves were willing to risk everything to escape their bondage. Slaveholders insisted that their slaves were happy, that they did not *wish* to be free. But runaway slaves made liars out of those slaveholders. From the very out-set slaves had run away when the chance arose. If they were recaptured and returned to slav-ery, they would run away again. They would hide in swamps, mail themselves in boxes to abolitionists—anything to escape the injustice of being someone's property. No slave is happy. It is impossible for those words to go together.

By the middle of the 1800s the make-believe was falling to pieces like a worn-out costume. The federal government, the government of the whole United States, tried to leave the decision of slavery to the individual states. But the notion of *United* States was becoming harder and harder to believe in. Not only was this make-believe about liberty and equality falling apart, but the Union itself was beginning to come apart at the seams.

★ ★ ★ ★ ★

THE RAIL-SPLITTER

WHEN ABRAHAM LINCOLN was a boy in the Kentucky wilderness, he didn't have much time for school. Life on a farm meant hard work and plenty of it for a strong boy. Lincoln grew to manhood without spending much time at a schoolroom desk. He had an education in splitting fence rails and plowing fields, but not much book learning. That is not to say that he wasn't a smart man—he

just wasn't an educated man, and there's a big difference.

The family moved from Kentucky to Indiana, and finally to Illinois when Lincoln was a young man. His first taste of leadership came when he volunteered in the Illinois militia, and was elected captain of his company. After that he decided he'd like to try his hand at politics. In 1832 he ran for a seat in the Illinois house of representatives. He failed. Two years later he ran again, and won. That was the first of four terms in a row.

It was while he was serving in the Illinois legislature that Lincoln decided he'd like to study to become a lawyer. He had a lawyer's logical mind, and he had a special knack for proving his side of an argument. Step by step by step, he could lay out the facts in a clear and uncomplicated way until soon enough he'd have everyone convinced. He was a natural persuader and a gifted storyteller. Years of farming had given him an appreciation for plain talk, and he would far rather earn his bread by arguing and debating than by splitting fence rails or plowing fields.

In some ways Lincoln was an unlikely person to succeed as a public speaker. He was tall and awkward and held himself in a hunched posture. He had a high, raspy voice and a backwoods Kentucky accent that made him sound like a country bumpkin. He tended to wave his hands around in the air as he spoke. He was not a good-looking man. Many people, when they saw him for the first time, had pretty low expectations.

But without fail his audiences perked up as they listened to what he actually *said* in that high and raspy voice. He was so sensible. So logical. So plainspoken. So funny. And so *smart*. If Abraham Lincoln had set out to prove that the sun shone at night and the moon was made of buttermilk biscuits, he probably could have talked people into believing it.

Instead, what he talked them into believing was that slavery had to be sorted out one way or another. It was time to stop pretending.

★ ★ ★ ★ ★

EXPANDING SLAVERY

LINCOLN'S POLITICAL CAREER soon took him to the United States Congress, where he served as a representative for Illinois. The federal capital was bustling with citizen politicians from every state in the Union. The air of Washington, D.C., buzzed with debate. During Lincoln's term in Congress the United States was at war with Mexico over Texas. There was a lot of territory beyond America's frontiers, and many of those territories wanted to become states and join the Union. But whether those new states would allow slavery or not was a question that sparked hot arguments in Congress. The pro-slavery Southern states wanted to allow the expansion of slavery. The antislavery Northern states wanted it outlawed in any territory that wanted to become a new state. Texas was a territory that already had slavery. Grabbing it from Mexico and making it a state would add another pro-slavery state to the Union.

Lincoln was against it. He was no fan of slavery, but he wasn't exactly an abolitionist, either. He wasn't on a crusade to abolish slavery throughout the United States. What he did care about was the law. And the way he read the law, the federal government had decided long ago to ban slavery in the territories.

So on one side of the debate were those who

felt the federal government had authority over the states on this issue. On the other side were those who felt that the states should get to decide for themselves. Legal thinkers hoped for a decision from the Supreme Court that could settle the question.

Finally the court did get a case.

But it didn't turn out the way the antislavery movement had hoped for.

Dred Scott was a Missouri slave who had lived, off and on, in several free states and territories, including Illinois. His owner was an army doctor, and Scott had moved with his owner to different army postings. After the doctor's death the widow continued to own Scott and live in Missouri. Scott went to court to claim his freedom. He claimed that because he had lived for a total of seven years in free states, he should be considered a free man.

FRANK LESLIE'S ILLUSTRATED NEWSPAPER

NEW YORK, MARCH 6, 1857.

Entered According to Act of Congress, in the year 1857, by Frank Leslie, in the Clerks office of the District Court for the Southern District

No. 82—VOL. IV

DRED SCOTT DECISION IS HANDED DOWN BY SUPREME COURT

Chief Justice Roger B. Taney today announced the Court's decision on the Dred S___ se. Taney and his fel___ held that when ___ Constitution ___ was written, ___ at slaves were ___ property, and ___ slaveholders have an ___ right to take their property ___ th them into the territories. The Fifth Amendment guarantees that no person "should be deprived of life, liberty or property without due process of law." Taney and the Court maintained any law that would abridge that Constitutional right would be, in ___ f, a violation of due process. The ___ that Congress had in point ___ d the Constitution by ___ Compromise. ___ ations

DRED SCOTT, PHOTOGRAPHED

ir rights

To the everlasting shame of the Supreme Court, it decided *against* Dred Scott. The property rights of the owner outweighed all others. To the Supreme Court, refusing to let the widow keep her property was the same as stealing from her. As her "property" Scott was denied his freedom.

The federal government had made a decision on slavery. For Dred Scott it was a personal disaster. But it meant disaster for the country as well.

CHAPTER SIX

★ ★ ★ ★ ★

THE DIVIDE

IN 1858 LINCOLN decided to run for the senate. His opponent was a nationally famous judge named Stephen Douglas. Douglas was in favor of letting the states decide for themselves whether to legalize slavery or not. The up-and-coming lawyer Lincoln challenged Douglas to a series of debates around their home state of Illinois. And because Douglas was so famous, newspapers from all around

the country printed the two candidates' speeches.

"A house divided against itself cannot stand," Lincoln said. A Union can't be two completely different things at the same time and not fall apart. It can't be both pro-slavery and antislavery. The law was the law, and it should apply equally to everyone in the country: Either slavery was legal, or it was not legal. Either slavery was a moral failure, or it was not. But it couldn't be a moral failure in Illinois and not over in the Oklahoma Territory. The logic was clear to Lincoln. He didn't see what legal right any of the Northern states had to outlaw something that was lawful in the new territories. It looked to him as though leaving the issue up to the states would end with one very undesirable result: slavery throughout the nation.

To his way of looking at it, that was what the Dred Scott decision meant. If Dred Scott was a slave in Illinois because he was a slave in Missouri, then what was to stop the man down the street from going to Georgia, buying a slave, and bringing him back to Illinois? Was Illinois a free state or was it not? Did the good people of Chicago and Springfield want their neighbors to own slaves? Lincoln believed the Supreme Court's decision was as wrong as wrong could be. He told the voters that if he won their ballot and went to the Senate, he would work to pass laws that would change what the Supreme Court had done. He would work to pass laws that made it clear that on the question of slavery, the federal government had power over the states.

He still wasn't talking about abolishing slavery where it already existed: In those states it was the law, and Lincoln the lawyer was an upholder of the law. But he was rock-solid sure that it could not be allowed to *spread*. Otherwise, sooner or later, the state of Illinois would wake up one morning and find itself a slave state. Stop the spread now, and soon enough, he was sure, slavery would just die out on its own. *Then* the nation would truly be blessed with universal freedom. It would finally live up to its promise and be a nation dedicated to the proposition that all men were created equal.

Lincoln didn't win the senate race, but with all the newspaper stories during the campaign, he had become *famous* for the power of his logical arguments. Lincoln was now known around the country. Known and, in many states, admired. Known and, in many states, hated. The pro-slavery forces were convinced he was getting ready to snatch their slaves and their whole way of life out from their grasp:

If he'd been the devil himself, they couldn't have hated him more. When the presidential campaign came around in 1860, Lincoln was ready to run for the highest office in the land.

The state government of South Carolina warned that if that gawky, raspy-voiced lawyer from Illinois won the presidency, it would secede from the Union—pack up and leave. There was no power on earth that would make them accept Abraham Lincoln as president.

Well, Lincoln won the presidency.

South Carolina voted to secede. Within weeks Mississippi, Florida, Alabama, Georgia, Louisiana, and Texas had followed it out the door. The South was now in open rebellion against the federal government.

Now we are engaged in a great civil war, testing whether that nation, or any nation so conceived and, so dedicated, can long endure.

CHAPTER SEVEN

★ ★ ★ ★ ★

BROTHER AGAINST BROTHER

LINCOLN HADN'T EVEN been inaugurated yet, and here he was faced with a rebellious upheaval of nearly half the country. On March 4, 1861, he was sworn in as president, and along with his oath of office he swore to protect the Union and its laws. In South Carolina, just over a month later, state troops fired on the federal garrison at Fort Sumter in Charleston's harbor.

The Civil War had begun.

Soon Virginia, Tennessee, Arkansas, North Carolina—even the Cherokee Nation—had joined the rebel cause. The new Confederate States of America declared Richmond, Virginia, their capital. At once they began to raise its army.

Lincoln was raising his army too. The Union must be preserved. The unlawful rebellion must be defeated.

It should have been over quickly. People expected it to be over quickly—over by Christmas at the latest. From Rhode Island to Minnesota, boys pouted in disappointment, sure that the fighting would be over before they ever had a chance to join up. After all, the North had a population of over twenty million people. The North also had industrial factories and plenty of railroads and ships for moving armies and supplies.

In the South, if you didn't count the slaves, there were only about nine million people, and they were not nearly so well supplied with factories and railroads and ships. By numbers alone the Union should have been able to squash that confederacy of rebel states before the leaves turned colors in the sugar hills of Vermont, before the geese flew over the lakes of Indiana, before the pumpkins grew ripe in Massachusetts, or before the apples fell off the trees in Ohio.

But to Lincoln's dismay it didn't work out that way.

North and South used the spring and early summer of 1861 to raise and train their armies. Here and there were small battles—skirmishes, really—that didn't prove anything one way or another. The first great clash came in July. There was a town a little ways south of Washington, D.C., called Manassas Junction, where a stream called

Bull Run simmered in the summer sun. It looked like the armies were going to meet head-on there.

Folks drove out from the capital in their carriages to see the fight, planning to be home by suppertime. There was an air of holiday, with flags flying and patriotic songs to sing like "Union Forever!" and "Star Spangled Banner." Photographers drove wagons equipped with darkrooms so they could take pictures of the victory. Ladies waved to the soldiers as they marched past in their new uniforms. "There's our senator!" called out a soldier from Connecticut, and the Union boys were thrilled to think they were about to whip the rebs in front of all the bigwigs from Washington. But when the battle turned into a defeat for the Union, the spectators turned and fled in terror, their carriages clogging the roads. Riderless horses galloped madly among running soldiers: The

FINISHED RR

NE N E

WARRENTON TURNPIKE

CUB RUN

BULL RUN

BURNSIDE

BEAUREGARD
JOHNSTON

NEW MARKET

SUDLEY ROAD

MANASSAS GAP RR

FIRST BATTLE OF
BULL RUN
JULY 21 1861

CONFEDERATE

UNION

Union army was skedaddling right alongside the civilians.

After the Battle of Bull Run both armies pulled back to bandage their wounds and review the situation. The battle was over, but the war wasn't, that was for sure. Maybe it *wouldn't* be over quite as fast as people had imagined. It no longer seemed like a thrilling, patriotic picnic. Folks were no longer so confident it would all be over by Christmas, and the country was beginning to feel a deep wound in its soul. This was brother fighting brother, American fighting American, Billy Yank firing at Johnny Reb. Was this what the glorious new nation had become? In Washington, Lincoln named a new general and told him to defeat the rebellion by taking Richmond, the Confederate capital. The Civil War was settling in for a good, long stay.

By the following summer, battles had been

fought in Virginia, Tennessee, Louisiana, and South Carolina, but the South was still not defeated and Richmond had not been invaded. The rebellion had not been put down. In fact the Union had been soundly beaten in a number of key battles, and Lincoln had to appoint another new general, one who would go ahead and march on Richmond. Confidence up North was wavering, and Britain was considering coming in on the side of the Confederacy: After all, if the American War of Independence was a just cause, why shouldn't the Southern states declare themselves independent of the Union?

There were some who suspected in 1862 that the Union might actually fail.

★ ★ ★ ★ ★

THE UNTAPPED ARMY

WHAT WERE THEY fighting for, anyway, those Union soldiers? What did they think they were protecting? It wasn't a war to free the slaves. The typical soldier from New York or Wisconsin wasn't risking his life for a black field hand on a Georgia cotton farm or for a cook on a Mississippi steamboat. If you asked, most of the Union soldiers would say they were fighting to preserve the Union, that the rebs were traitors to a lawful government and had to be punished. If the South was allowed to secede, then the Union—the nation created by their founding fathers—would be finished. If the South was allowed to secede, then any state could pull out at any time. There would be no such thing as a Union governed by the people for the people. There would be no such thing as a Union of laws. The Union had to endure, and that was all there was to it.

No, most of them weren't fighting to free the slaves.

But Lincoln knew, and a growing number of other people knew, that protecting the Union was meaningless. Meaningless, that is, if it wasn't really a nation where all men were created equal. If the Union didn't hope to free the slaves, then why was it worth fighting for? Who really wanted to die for a meaningless idea? Why did this Union deserve to endure? Was it just about punishing the South for wanting to be independent? Was that worth all the death and destruction?

In the South the slaves themselves knew what the war was about. They knew better than many up in the North, and sooner, that it all came down to one thing: equality for all, the blessings of liberty for all. With fighting spirit among the Union troops low and recruitment dwindling, Lincoln turned his eyes to the great untapped army of black slaves. *They* would be willing to fight for their freedom. Freeing the slaves would do two things: It would bring millions of new soldiers into the Union Army, and it would finally make good on the promise of the founding fathers.

But were white soldiers willing to let this war become a war to free the slaves, a war for emancipation? After all, some of the states that had stayed in the Union were slave-holding states—Maryland, for example, and West Virginia. There was a very real fear that Union soldiers would desert the army, quit, and go home if Lincoln made a move toward emancipation.

As 1862 wore on, Lincoln debated what to do. He was a lawyer, and he had to obey the law. In the slaveholding loyal Union states, the slaves were slaves by law. Legally, he could do nothing about them. Freeing them would require new laws passed by the federal government, and right now the federal government was in an uproar.

But the slaves in the rebel states—*they* were a different matter. Those states were traitors. Those states were in defiance of the lawful government and its lawfully elected president. Lincoln could, by presidential decree as a wartime emergency act, *free* the slaves in those states. He could free *those* slaves. Not *all* slaves. Not the slaves in the states loyal to the Union. But it would be a start.

When the time was right.

If only the Union could score a great victory against the Confederacy! The North was badly in need of a triumph to raise its spirits and prove that right and justice were on its side. By September the rebel army was actually on Union soil, marching into Maryland. If such a small and ill-equipped army could invade the powerful North, maybe the Union didn't deserve to win this fight, after all.

Lincoln swore to himself that if his army could stop the advance of the Confederate invasion, he would take action. The much-needed victory came at Antietam Creek in Maryland. Billy Yank halted Johnny Reb's onward rush and pushed it back. Now Lincoln was ready to honor his promise.

"God has decided in favor of the slaves," Lincoln told his cabinet officials. On January 1, 1863, Abraham Lincoln signed the Emancipation Proclamation. With one signature, Lincoln freed the millions of slaves in the Confederacy. The Union was now, truly, something worth fighting—and dying—for.

We are met on a great battlefield of that war. We have come to dedicate a portion of that field as a final resting place for those who here gave their lives that that nation might live. It is altogether fitting and proper that we should do this. But in a larger sense we cannot dedicate—we cannot consecrate—we cannot hallow this ground. The brave men, living and dead, who struggled, here, have consecrated it far above our poor power to add or detract.

CHAPTER NINE

★ ★ ★ ★ ★

BAREFOOT SOLDIERS

BY THE SUMMER of 1863 the war was two years old. Boys who had joined up as green and untested recruits were now battle-hard veterans. Virginia and Maryland were pockmarked with holes and littered with cartridge shells. Trees blasted by cannon fire leaned like broken gravestones. Villages lay in smoking ruins. Farmers trying to work their fields turned pale and wept as they unearthed bones and shreds of uniforms.

The commander of the Confederate army, General Robert E. Lee, was suffering. Because he had started out with a much smaller army, he couldn't afford a long war. He was losing more soldiers to disease than to battle, and he feared that if the fight continued another two years, he would have no army to fight with. The factory-poor South was also running short of supplies for Lee's army. They were low on uniforms, guns, ammunition, and horses. Many soldiers were marching barefoot. Scavenging food from the countryside was the only way for most men to get enough to eat. This war had to end soon.

In order to force a showdown, Lee began to lead his army up into Union territory again. If he could get into a position north of Washington, it would force the Union army to come after him in order to defend the capital. Under

Lee's command the rebel army moved into Pennsylvania.

Both Union and Confederate forces made their way across Pennsylvania as June drew to a close. Patrols and scouts from each side probed this way and that, seeking the enemy's main force. Then someone in Lee's army reported that there was a stockpile of shoes in a nearby town. Shoes! That was just what the tired and footsore Confederate soldiers needed! On July 1 a division of Confederate forces entered Gettysburg, Pennsylvania, looking for shoes.

They found two Union cavalry brigades already there.

CHAPTER TEN

★ ★ ★ ★ ★

A TERRIBLE INDEPENDENCE DAY

THE BATTLE BEGAN at once with scattered fighting at the crossroads. Word spread rapidly that the armies had met, and every division in the area began streaming toward Gettysburg. The people who lived in the town watched in horror while cavalry officers galloped past and teams of horses pulled cannons into position. None of the residents knew what to do. Run away or stay in the house? Hide in the cellar or risk getting caught in the crossfire on the road? The air was already thick with gunsmoke, but as more and more divisions arrived, one thing was quite clear. The town had been chosen for a terrible fate. By the next morning there were 150,000 troops awaiting battle orders in and around Gettysburg.

For the next two days the fighting continued. It was desperate on both sides. Each tried to gain high ground. First a division of Union troops was winning over here. Then a division of Confederate troops broke through the line over there. The advantage passed back and forth, and all the while, the ground shook with explosions. Bugle calls and the rattle of drums added to the thunder of gunfire. Screams of shot horses, screams of shot men, and screams of officers struggling to give orders increased the confusion. It was two days of nightmare.

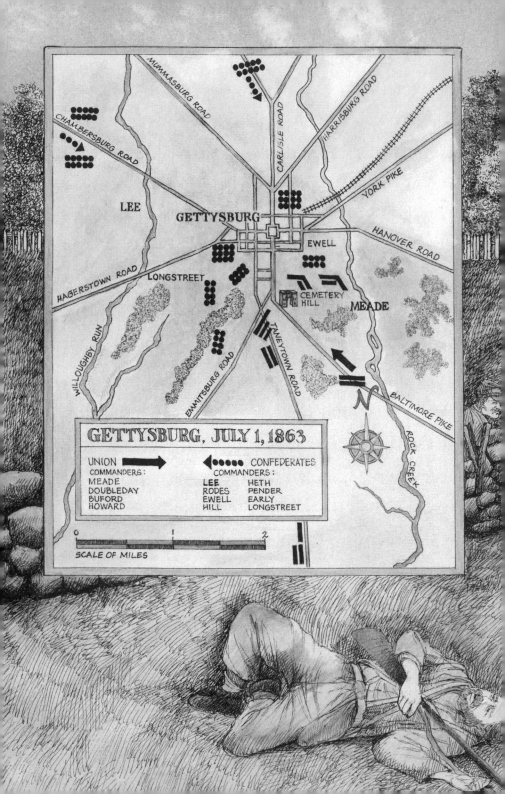

The dead and wounded lay in heaps on the ground, some still clutching a rifle or a flag or a comrade's hand. Houses were taken over as field hospitals, and blood ran down the staircases in streams. Lee's losses were close to 20,000 men, and he knew he could not afford it. In a last desperate effort, he sent three divisions under General Pickett to charge the center of the Union line, high on a ridge. The federal position was too well armed and protected to defeat. They rained bullets down onto the advancing rebel troops, and Pickett's Charge took such heavy casualties that it qualified as a sheer disaster. By the end of the day on July 3, Lee's army was in retreat and the invasion of the North was over.

The war wasn't over, however. If the Union commander, General Meade, had chased Lee and kept the fight going, it might have ended

with a final, crushing defeat of the rebel army. As it was, Meade felt nearly as whipped as Lee, and he decided not to give chase.

A full moon rose that night on twenty-three thousand dead and injured Union soldiers, and twenty-eight thousand dead and wounded Confederates; in the moonlight, the ground seemed to tremble and twitch with the agonized movements of the dying men. As the sun rose on July 4, 1863, the residents of Gettysburg came creeping out of their cellars and looked over the ruins of their town. It was a terrible Independence Day. The Union had won the battle and might well have tipped the balance of the whole war. But the fight for freedom had turned Gettysburg into a cemetery.

The next day brought rain, which washed the upturned faces of the men still lying on the field. But the cleanup had only just begun.

★ ★ ★ ★ ★

THE CEMETERY

GENERAL MEADE DID not linger in Gettysburg to bury his dead soldiers—or the Confederate dead. In the heat of summer it was left to the people of Gettysburg to take care of the awful, horrible mess. Thousands of dead horses and mules were burned in giant bonfires. But the soldiers—the soldiers had to be given decent burials, and as fast as possible. Already the broiling July heat was causing them to decay. The governor of Pennsylvania appointed a prominent Gettysburg citizen named David Wills to oversee the operation. Right away he purchased a portion of the battlefield—seventeen acres of it—for a military cemetery. Then the burials began.

There was no time to sort the dead by army division or by state. The bodies had to be buried almost where they lay. If a personal letter, Bible, or other piece of identification could be found on the body, the soldier's name and regiment was written on a board and pounded into the ground at the head of the grave. When possible, rebel soldiers were separated from the Union dead, but sometimes it was impossible to tell. Gettysburg had become the final resting place for soldiers from every state in the nation.

It was clear from the beginning that these thousands of dead soldiers deserved some kind

of funeral service. The battle had been the largest and bloodiest in American history. Just as important, it had been the key to breaking the Confederacy. The war wasn't over yet, but in the public's opinion Gettysburg had been the critical battle. These soldiers had given their lives so that the nation might live. Sacrifice of that kind required a ceremony. It required speeches.

Making a speech was one of the most common ways to honor an occasion in those days. At that time speeches were long and wordy, filled with poetic language and historical references. People were accustomed to standing in crowds for *hours* to listen to speeches. An occasion as important as this one obviously required speeches: It was absolutely fitting and proper to do so. Work on the burial ground continued throughout the summer while Wills planned a great ceremony to dedicate the cemetery. The ceremony would consecrate the ground and make it holy: It would change Gettysburg from a bloody battlefield to a hallowed monument.

The star of the show would be Edward Everett of Massachusetts. He was a master speech-maker, an orator supreme. He had made speeches to dedicate monuments at Revolutionary War sites, and was considered the perfect person for the Gettysburg ceremony. He checked his schedule, and calculated how long it would take him to write an oration worthy of the day. He could be ready on November 19.

Everyone wanted to be there. Everyone knew it would be a memorable event, even a historical one. Everyone wanted to be able to say, "I was there when Edward Everett dedicated the Gettysburg Cemetery." Throughout the Northern states, politicians and citizens alike made plans to attend the ceremony in November.

On the second of November, Wills sent a letter to President Lincoln. In it he wrote:

These grounds will be consecrated and set apart to this sacred purpose by appropriate ceremonies. . . . Edward Everett will deliver the oration. I am authorized by the governors of the different States to invite you to be present, and to participate in these ceremonies. . . . It is the desire that, after the oration, you, as Chief Executive of the nation, formally set apart these grounds to their sacred use by a few appropriate remarks. It will be a source of great gratification to the many widows and orphans that have been made almost friendless by the Great Battle here, to have you here personally. . . . We hope you will be able to be present to perform this last solemn act to the soldiers dead on this battlefield.

The ceremony was just over two weeks away.

Of course, the president's schedule was pretty busy. The war was still unfinished and he had a country in turmoil to lead. Some people were still not convinced that this war should be about slavery and freedom, so politics kept the president at his desk until long after dark, day after day. But Lincoln would make the time to be present at the ceremony, and he would be glad to make "a few appropriate remarks."

The world will little note, nor long remember, what we say here, but it can never forget what they did here. It is for us, the living, rather to be dedicated here to the unfinished work which they have, thus far, so nobly carried on. It is rather for us to be here dedicated to the great task remaining before us—that from these honored dead we take increased devotion to that cause for which they here gave the last full measure of devotion—that we here highly resolve that these dead shall not have died in vain; that this nation shall have a new birth of freedom; and that government of the people, by the people, for the people, shall not perish from the earth.

★ ★ ★ ★ ★

THE BIG EVENT

THE PRESIDENT WAS already at work on his speech. The big event would be covered in all the newspapers, and thousands of people would be there in person. It was important to seize the opportunity to get across his message about the war. The fight wasn't over yet, and the Union needed a boost of confidence to keep at it until the very end. His few appropriate remarks would have to hit just the right note.

Lincoln's secretary studied the train schedules: Washington to Baltimore, Baltimore to Gettysburg. He informed the president that they could leave Washington at six in the morning and be in Gettysburg by noon. That would give them two hours to visit the cemetery before the two o'clock dedication.

Now, no matter how close Gettysburg was to Washington, D.C., there was a war on. Lincoln knew that even in peacetime, trains could be delayed or canceled. Two hours to spare just wouldn't be enough. He didn't want to risk getting there too late. "I do not like this arrangement," he wrote in a memo. "By the slightest accident we fail entirely."

When Wills had invited Lincoln to speak, he had also attached a private note. "As the hotels in our town will be crowded and in confusion . . . I write to invite you to stop with me." This was a much more sensible plan.

So the president took the train to Gettysburg the night before the ceremony. He found the town flooded with visitors. Hotels were indeed crowded and in confusion, and gravediggers were frantically tidying up at the cemetery. Bands played patriotic music in the streets. Small groups of men and women broke into song: "Yankee Doodle Dandy" and "The Battle Hymn of the Republic" brought tears to many eyes. Wounded veterans of the battle were greeted as heroes. Then word got out that the president was at Wills's house. A crowd gathered, singing and calling out to Lincoln to speak.

The president, finished with his dinner, gave them a friendly answer. "I appear before you, fellow citizens, merely to thank you for this compliment. . . . That you would hear me . . .

make a speech. I do not appear before you for the purpose of doing so, and for several substantial reasons. The most substantial of these is that I have no speech to make."

Loud laughter broke out in the crowd, but Lincoln continued. "In my position it is somewhat important that I should not say foolish things—"

"If you can help it!" someone shouted out, and there were more guffaws.

"It very often happens that the only way to help it is to say nothing at all," Lincoln went on in his backwoods drawl, and the boisterous crowd laughed again. "Believing that is my present condition this evening, I must beg of you to excuse me from addressing you further."

That was all the crowd would hear from Abraham Lincoln that night. He had a lot of

work to do before bedtime. There were tele-
grams to answer and war dispatches to catch
up on. He also had to meet with his secretaries, who had been gathering political news
from the visiting senators and governors.

The morning gave the president his first
chance to view the battleground and cemetery.
He rode out in a carriage and saw what he could
in the brief time he had. By eleven o'clock the
guests of honor and other bigwigs of the ceremony had to get ready for the procession. The
crowd of spectators would mostly be on foot,
tramping the short half mile from town to the
graveyard where a temporary stage had been set
up. But the speakers were to go on horseback on
a route around the huge crowd and come to the
platform from behind.

There was a bright November sky above.
The cool weather was helping to keep down

the smell of all those bodies so hastily buried. Lincoln sat astride the horse assigned to him, dressed in black from head to toe—except for his white gloves. Photographers were setting up their cameras, ready to record the big event.

At last the procession began to move. The guests of honor made their slow and solemn way, passing one spot and then another where soldiers had fought and died in July.

Music began the ceremony, and then the crowd was led in a long prayer by the Reverend T. H. Stockton. The marine band played. In the crowd ladies adjusted their shawls. Men too old to fight glanced at the uniformed soldiers in their midst and wished they were younger. Small children were shushed. It was time for the oration.

Edward Everett strode to the front of the

platform. In his hand was the thick stack of papers that was his speech. He placed it on a small table, and then began.

"Standing beneath this serene sky, overlooking these broad fields now reposing from the labors of the waning year, the mighty Alleghanies dimly towering before us, the graves of our brethren beneath our feet, it is with hesitation that I raise my poor voice to break the eloquent silence of God and Nature. But the duty to which you have called me must be performed;—grant me, I pray you, your indulgence and your sympathy."

And he continued to perform that duty for the next two hours. Step by step, he led the crowd through the history of the conflict. Day by day, he relived for them the bloody battle. He pointed out the sites that could be seen from where he stood, giving a blow-by-blow description of everything that had happened.

He compared the Battle of Gettysburg to battles from ancient Greek and Roman history. He mentioned every heroic deed. He mentioned every state in the Union with regiments at the battle. He described the movements of the enemy. He left nothing out. Finally, he came to the end.

"Wheresoever throughout the civilized world the accounts of this great warfare are read, and down to the latest period of recorded time, in the glorious annals of our common country, there will be no brighter page than that which relates the Battles of Gettysburg."

By now the late autumn sun was dipping toward the horizon. A hymn followed Everett's speech. The crowd shifted somewhat. People commented solemnly to each other that it had been a fine and inspiring oration. The next item on the program was "Dedicatory Remarks by the President of the United States." Already the spectators had been standing for nearly three hours; they prepared themselves for another typical, wordy speech.

The president walked to the front of the platform. He had two small sheets of notepaper in his hand. "Four score and seven years ago, our fathers brought forth, upon this continent, a new nation," he began, and his high, shrill voice carried all the way to the back of the crowd. "Conceived in liberty, and dedicated to the proposition that all men are created equal." As he spoke, the audience broke in repeatedly to applaud his words. Even with the interruptions it didn't take him much more than three minutes to read the whole speech. Without interruption it would have taken a slow reader less than two to complete. When the president finished his "few appropriate remarks," his listeners thanked him with more applause, and he returned to his seat.

More music. Another prayer. It was all over.

People turned and began to make their way out of the cemetery. The crowd had had a full day.

★ ★ ★ ★ ★

WHAT DID
HE SAY?

EVEN AS THEY walked back into town, people were wondering: What had they just witnessed? What had they just heard? What did he say? Lincoln might have said that the world would take little notice of what was said at the ceremony. But it was already clear to people that they had just heard something remarkable. In three minutes, Lincoln had turned the cemetery dedication upside down.

He had not once mentioned Gettysburg by name.

He had not once mentioned the enemy.

He hadn't mentioned slavery, or states' rights.

He had not mentioned any of the states by name, or even the name of the country!

Instead he talked about liberty. He talked about dying for liberty. He talked about giving the very last drop, the very last *measure* of devotion to the cause of liberty. He talked about continuing the struggle, because the work remained unfinished.

He had resolved that those honored dead would not have died in vain.

He had resolved that the country would be born over again.

He had resolved that the last eighty-seven years of inequality should be erased, like a mistake on the chalkboard. They would go back to the beginning again, and have a *new* birth of freedom.

He had resolved that democracy—government of the people, for the people, and by the people—would not die. Soldiers might die. But true democracy would not.

Abraham Lincoln hadn't dedicated a cemetery that day. *He had dedicated the whole war.*

CHAPTER FOURTEEN

★ ★ ★ ★ ★

THE MYTH

IT DIDN'T TAKE long for stories to spring up around Lincoln's Gettysburg Address. Some people said that the photographers had taken too long getting their cameras set up to take the president's picture, and that he was done before they could get a shot. Rumors spread that he had written the speech on the train on the back of an envelope—no, he had written it the night before the ceremony—no, he had written it while listening to Edward Everett's oration—no, he made it up on the spot. It was as if people wanted to believe that magic had happened before their very eyes.

It's true, Lincoln wrote the speech quickly: in just two weeks. But when he stood on the platform on that November afternoon, he had his finished speech, written in his own handwriting on stationery from his own office. From the moment he had left Washington for Gettysburg until almost the moment he gave the speech, Lincoln was busy working with his secretaries on other official business. He may have tinkered with it again after his arrival in Gettysburg, but there would have been no time for him to write a speech, even such a short one. And besides, it was too serious an occasion. Lincoln was not the sort of person to leave such an important speech to the last minute. He had been asked to make a few appropriate remarks, not a few casual words off the top of his head.

Back in Washington the president received a short note from Everett. "I should be glad if I could flatter myself that I came as near the central idea of the occasion in two hours as you did in two minutes."

Within days he had a request from Wills, in Gettysburg. Could he please have the original copy of the speech to keep with the documents related to the event? It wasn't long before other people were asking for autographed copies of the speech. Lincoln sent a copy to a fund-raising auction to aid wounded soldiers in January, and he sent others out later. It had already become one of the most famous speeches of a war filled with speeches.

It has since become one of the most famous

speeches of all time. Lincoln said "the world will little note nor long remember what we say here."

It was the only part he got wrong.

★ ★ ★ ★ ★

WHICH SPEECH DID HE WRITE AND WHICH SPEECH DID HE SPEAK?

Four score and seven years ago, our fathers brought forth, upon this continent, a new nation, conceived in liberty, and dedicated to the proposition that all men are created equal. Now we are engaged in a great civil war, testing whether that nation, or any nation so conceived, and so dedicated, can long endure. We are met on a great battlefield of that war. We have come to dedicate a portion of that field as a final resting place for those who here gave their lives that that nation might live. It is altogether fitting and proper that we should do this. But in a larger sense we cannot dedicate—we cannot consecrate—we cannot hallow this ground. The brave men, living and dead, who struggled, here, have consecrated it far above our poor power to add or detract. The world will little note, nor long remember, what we say here, but it can never forget what they did here. It is for us, the living, rather to be dedicated here to the unfinished work which they have, thus far, so nobly carried on. It is rather for us to be here dedicated to the great task remaining before us—that from these honored dead we take increased devotion to that cause for which they here gave the last full measure of devotion—that we here highly resolve that these dead shall not have died in vain; that this nation shall have a new birth of freedom; and that government of the people, by the people, for the people, shall not perish from the earth.

The handwritten speech that Lincoln read was sent to Wills, and Lincoln and his secretary made additional handwritten copies for Edward Everett and others. Four different newspaper reporters taking down the speech as they heard it at Gettysburg printed it in their papers. There were very small variations in each version, which goes to show that in the days when many things were written by hand, slight changes were a common mistake. It is no longer possible to know which was the *exact* text Lincoln read at Gettysburg that day, and most of the drafts and copies of the speech have long since disappeared. We can't even know for sure that Lincoln read exactly from the paper he held before him on the platform, or whether he changed a word here and there on the spur of the moment. The version used here is in the Library of Congress, and is believed to be the earliest copy still in existence.

BIBLIOGRAPHY

★ ★ ★ ★ ★

FOR MY UNDERSTANDING of this speech and its significance I owe a large debt to Garry Wills's masterful book, *Lincoln at Gettysburg: The Words That Remade America.* Other books and websites that were useful are listed below.

Long, E. B., with Barbara Long. *The Civil War Day by Day: An Almanac 1861–1865.* Garden City, New York: Doubleday, 1971.

Ward, Geoffrey C. *The Civil War: An Illustrated History.* New York: Alfred A. Knopf, 1990.

Wheeler, Richard. *Voices of the Civil War.* New York: Penguin, 1976.

Wills, Garry. *Lincoln at Gettysburg: The Words That Remade America.* New York: Simon & Schuster, 1992.

Websites:

Library of Congress—
Gettysburg Address Exhibition
http://www.loc.gov/exhibits/gadd

America's Story from America's Library:
Jump Back in Time
http://www.americaslibrary.gov

Library of Congress Historical Documents—
The Declaration of Independence
http://www.memory.loc.gov/const/declar.html

Abraham Lincoln Online
www.abrahamlincolnonline.org

Lincoln-Douglas Debates
on History Channel Online
www.history.com/topics/lincoln-douglas-debates

JENNIFER ARMSTRONG has always been captivated by history. Her more than one hundred books for children and teens include many historical fiction and nonfiction titles, including *Photo by Brady: A Picture of the Civil War.* She lives in Saratoga Springs, New York, with her daughter.